A Friendly Society Records

LOGAN, Roger
friendly Society Records

Roger Logan

D1354126

334. 70941

Published by
The Federation of Family History Societies (Publications) Ltd
Units 15-16 Chesham Ind. Est., Oram Street, Bury, Lancs BL9 6EN

First published 2000

ISBN 1-86006 115 X

Printed and bound by The Alden Group, Oxford and Northampton

Contents

List of Illustrations

Acknowledgements

Suffolk County Record Office for Illustrations 1 and 2.

Independent Order of Oddfellows (Manchester Unity), South London
District for Illustration 4.

Ancient Order of Foresters Friendly Society, Executive Council for
the remaining illustrations.

Introduction

In recent years the role of Friendly Societies during the 19th century has come back into public consciousness as politicians of all parties have looked to the past in efforts to find alternatives to the "welfare state" and its associated values. As awareness of their activities has developed so has an appreciation of the value of records which can provide family historians with the opportunity to supplement better known sources to extend their knowledge of their forefathers' lives. From Friendly Societies' own records, as well as those from other sources having a bearing on their activities, an enlarged knowledge and understanding of the part played by an individual in both his/her local community and his/her own family life can be gained.

The Friendly Society movement of the 19th century developed into one of three significant working peoples' institutions. Together with the co-operative societies and trade unions, friendly societies operated on the principle of mutual self help, binding people together with the objective of a common purpose, success being achieved through their own combined efforts. It was not unusual for someone prominent in the administration of one to play a similarly active role in one of the other organisations.

To assist family historians to benefit fully from this *"Introduction to Friendly Society Records"* the following is a brief account of the origins, objectives and evolution of friendly societies into outstandingly practical organisations. So successful, in fact, that their absorption into a state administered scheme, and their own ultimate decline, became inevitable.

The aims of Friendly, or Benefit, Societies were first given legal identification in Great Britain by an Act of Parliament which received Royal Assent on 21st June 1793. Many existing societies, however, pre-dated the Act, some by up to 50, perhaps 75, years. Authorising *'any number of persons ... to form themselves into ... Societies of good fellowship ... for the mutual relief and maintenance ... in old age, sickness and infirmity or for the relief of the widows and children of deceased members',* the Act prescribed the basic laws under which such societies could operate.

Whilst figures are imprecise, it can be said that by the first decade of the nineteenth century local friendly societies were active across the whole of

Great Britain. In England alone it has been estimated that by 1803 some 38% of all families were connected to a friendly society. This level varied from 79% in Lancashire to 10% in Hampshire. As to who the members of late 18th and early 19th century friendly societies were, this is one of the exciting and important areas of research now being undertaken, resulting, it is to be hoped, in an increase in data of interest to family historians.

Around 1813 a new development began to become established in the nature of friendly societies. Instead of a society having a membership and identity based solely on its location or trade, a new structure emerged whereby individual groups acted in association with others under a degree of centralised control. Thus emerged the Affiliated Societies or "Orders", e.g. the Independent Order of Oddfellows (Manchester Unity), the Ancient Order of Foresters, the Independent Order of Rechabites, etc.

Within these Orders, local units retained much of their autonomy and independence whilst conceding to a central elected body some overall elements of policy making and administration. Known as "secret Orders" as a consequence of their having passwords and signs known only to members, the majority of Orders operated, with increasing success, during the 1830s and 1840s. This was achieved despite their not being registered or enrolled under the Friendly Societies Acts, leaving them unrecognised in law, and consequently susceptible to suffering unrecoverable financial losses. This could occur on the failure of a bank where a society's funds might be invested or, more closely to home, on the occasion of a Secretary or Treasurer succumbing to temptation and absconding with members' money. Fortunately such instances were few, and clearly until the acceptance of the Friendly Societies Act by Orders, the membership trusted to the honesty of officers.

Whilst other financial benefits were available, payments at death, for example, it was the principal function of friendly societies, local or branches of Orders, for over two centuries to offer the man and woman financial support in times of sickness. By way of an example, the Ancient Order of Foresters, one of the two giant friendly society Orders, paid out, from branch funds, between 1900 and 1911, **average amounts** of over **£600,000** per annum in sickness benefit, and **£135,000** in death benefits, truly astounding amounts of financial support reaching many tens of thousands of families throughout the United Kingdom.

The Orders varied in strength in different parts of the country at different times. A survey carried out by the Foresters in 1904 found that in many areas of over 10,000 people there were no Courts (branches) or Districts. In Liverpool, with a population of over 684,000, there were no Foresters where, in the formative years of the 1830s and 1840s there were thousands. The same was true of Rochdale, once a heartland of the Order. Oddfellows of the Manchester Unity could be found in all the counties of England by the mid 1840s, although those belonging to other Oddfellows Unities, many of which periodically splintered off, tended to be more localised. Some places never were 'colonised' and further research is needed to produce a comprehensive account of the relative geographical strengths of the Orders during the 19th century.

By the beginning of the 20th century not only friendly societies but employers, trade unions and commercial insurance companies were all providing financial benefits for spells of sickness, a situation which was recognised by the state when in 1911 the Liberal government assumed responsibility for the provision of support for at least some of those too ill to attend work. Large friendly societies, along with other major providers of sickness benefits, were designated as "Approved Societies" under the National Insurance Act, and as a consequence the Orders had both 'state' and 'voluntary' members. Many local societies which had maintained their presence in villages and towns, ceased to exist, some choosing to become branches of one of the larger Orders.

This arrangement lasted until 1948, when, with the introduction of the welfare state, friendly societies were abruptly removed from the state scheme of health insurance provision, although voluntary membership continued. On that basis the major Orders such as the Foresters and Oddfellows continue to function today, within the onerous constraints placed upon them by Friendly Society and Financial Services Acts.

But friendly societies were far from simply being about money. The friendly society movement, as it evolved during the 19th century, constituted a definite culture, underpinned by ethical codes, by ideals of service, exemplified by democratic, educational practices. The significance of the Orders in the fabric of society was recognised by the eminent statesman, W.E. Gladstone (himself a member of the Loyal Order of Ancient Shepherds (Ashton Unity)), declaring in 1878 that

"I see in institutions of this kind not only the means of increasing thrift, not only the means for securing and elevating the position of the working class as a class; but I see that which is more important than any of these things; namely the promoting of the education of the individual mind... From morning till night, [educational] influence is affecting your whole life, and this and kindred societies are a very important part of this education."

Above all, the Friendly Society movement of the 19th century depended on individual commitment and involvement offering tremendous scope for personal "self-improvement". From the records of individual societies an appreciation of this can be gained.

AVAILABILITY OF RECORDS

There is currently no one central source of information providing details about where all friendly societies' records are held. At a conference arranged by the Open University in the Spring of 1999 proposals for a survey of extant societies records were agreed; however, for the present, family historians will need to develop their own "database" of useful sources for the nineteenth century.

The pre-eminent source is the Royal Commission on Historical Manuscripts (RCHM) which maintains the computerised National Register of Archives (NRA) database. The classification of Masonic and non-health insurance related societies means that the total number of entries under friendly societies is exaggerated. However to assist the family historian to assess the likelihood of the survival of known records for his or her own county, analyses of entries for England, Scotland and Wales are shown in Appendices A, B and C. The NRA database is accessible by fax, e-mail and has a website (http://www.hmc.gov.uk). For those intending to use the facility the main code number for friendly society records is 26 and the sub code 3.

The NRA listings are of recorded survivals. However it is clear from the experience of many researchers that much material is held in local, county or private archives which is unclassified and not generally known about. The key to identifying the survival of such records is persistence, a characteristic already well known to family historians.

8

Community or Village Societies

Research has firmly established that, by 1750, friendly societies were being formed with increasing regularity in local communities throughout England, Scotland and Wales. In the East Riding of Yorkshire, for example, the market town of Howden, near Goole, contained a friendly society established in 1751. Further south, in Surrey there was a society in Kingston as early as 1738. Such societies remained active until early in the 20th century, operating alongside both Orders and other forms of benefit societies.

TYPES OF RECORD

The prime source of our detailed knowledge of these early friendly societies and their members comes about as a direct consequence of the 1793 Friendly Societies Act. Requirements were laid down for a number of things such as the establishment of a body of rules, with their confirmation by Justices of the Peace, the deposit of financial bonds for certain 'officers' of societies with magistrates, and the registration of certain other specific activities. This Act, along with its successors, prescribed a framework of documented transactions relating to the operation of registered friendly societies during the 19th century. From these can be derived many personal names, occupations and sometimes addresses.

RULES

The requirement to register rules under the 1793 Act was a measure saught by some friendly societies keen to place themselves under the protection of the law. Coincidentally this enabled the authorities to implement their own agenda of identifying and monitoring the activities of unregulated groups meeting across Great Britain during the prevalent climate of fear arising from the revolutionary events and social upheavals taking place in Europe.

The Rules themselves contain much of interest to social and economic historians but are not enormously useful to family historians. Names of officers and members can sometimes be found together with larger lists of names. An example of the latter can be seen in rules of a local friendly society located in Putney, Surrey. Along with the set of 43 rules laid down for the operation of the society there is a list of 63 names of members, some marked with a cross, bearing the date 1799 at the top.

The most substantial collection of Rules and amendments relating to local friendly societies is to be found at the Public Record Office in Kew. They can also be found in the British Library, County Record Offices and University libraries.

FINANCIAL BONDS

The deposit of financial bonds for individuals associated with the operation of the early village societies is a major source of personal information. The 1793 Act specified that, for all officers appointed to any position of trust involving handling money, they should "become bound with two sufficient Sureties." Bonds are to be found in County Record Offices.

Trustee's bond

From the financial contributions made to a friendly society, it became possible for money not needed for the everyday running of the organisation to be invested, either in private Securities or in Public Stocks or Funds, thus producing interest for the society to improve its benefits. Responsibility for investing the money lay with trustees or stockholders, who were required to appear in front of a Justice of the Peace to supply information about themselves, usually names, addresses and occupations.

On the 17th of July 1805 the three trustees of the Friends to Peace Friendly Society, which met at the Ship, in New Street, St John, Southwark appeared before the Justice of the Peace, Charles John Lawson to deposit their bond in the sum of £200. The three trustees names, addresses and occupations were given (see below), usefully complementing other known information about these Bermondsey inhabitants.

John Scott	Dockhead, Bermondsey	Rope maker
John Hinckley	Mill Street, Bermondsey	Boat builder
John Doll	Russell Street, Bermondsey	Leather dresser

Secretary's bond

Less common than Trustee's bonds are Secretary's bonds. Similarly, female societies were not so numerous as those for men. An example of a combination of both relates to the Banstead and Chipstead Female Benefit Society. Its meeting place was the Sunday School room at Banstead. Before the same Justice as the previous example, Charles Lawson, the Secretary, Ann Aubertin, spinster, was on the 6th December 1806 bound in the sum of £30 with Peter Aubertin, Clerk and Daniel Lambert, Gentleman.

Landlord's bond

The great majority of community/trade friendly societies met on licensed premises. The landlord of those premises was often a key figure, not only providing facilities for meetings to be held but also as the treasurer, or keeper of the funds and other important documents. It was essential to minimise the possibility of any funds being absconded with, so a bond between the landlord and the officers was drawn up and executed before a magistrate.

An example of this can be found in records relating to a bond made in May 1810 in connection with the Southwark Assurance Friendly Society which met at The Rose in Russell Street, Bermondsey. The landlord was Charles Palmer and on 1st May 1810 he was bound in the sum of £100, along with Robert Campion, presumably his partner, to the two Stewards of the Society, Simon Wale and William Simmonds.

CERTIFICATES

Among the provisions of the 1793 Act, one in the contemporary social context was important. This enabled a friendly society member to gain exemption from the Law relating to legal settlement (see *An Introduction to Poor Law Documents before 1834,* Anne Cole, Federation of Family History Societies, 1993). The means of doing this was to obtain a certificate for presentation to the Churchwardens and Overseers of the Poor where the member lived. The process involved getting the Certificate signed by two of the officers of the society. These signatures were themselves attested to by two witnesses. The Certificate was endorsed by a Justice of the Peace, certifying that one of the witnesses had sworn an oath before him, confirming that he (the witness) had seen the two officers sign the

Certificate. An example of such a document is depicted in Illustration 1. This type of document is to be found in record offices in many parts of the country.

ADMINISTRATIVE RECORDS

Meeting place removals

Some transactions did take place which resulted in a useful record of personal names being made. One such took place in July 1801 when the members of the Royal Oak Benefit Society in Rotherhithe met in a general meeting to request the production of a bond held by Francis Lawson, Justice of the Peace. This bond referred to the landlord of the King and Queen Dock house, Daniel Swallow. As a result of his bankruptcy the Society decided to transfer its meeting place, and equally importantly, custody of its box or chest, in which were the valuables belonging to the Society, to the Boatswain and Pall, Rotherhithe.

Appended to the document drawn up for the JP is a list of current members, some 47 in all. Such a comprehensive record has many uses, but for family historians with ancestors in Rotherhithe it provides an interesting source of information.

Application forms, cash books, and membership lists

With the *raison d'être* of local friendly societies being the financial support of members and their families at times of illness and death, a substantial volume of internal documentation was required in their administration. This fact, together with their continued formation throughout the 19th century has resulted in the survival of known records in many record offices (see Appendices). The usefulness of a particular surviving record can only be determined by individual examination. It is clear that a membership list of a specific society in a given location covering a particular period could well confirm the membership of an antecedent. It will always be worth making an enquiry at the record office.

[Friendly Society Certificate.]

To the Churchwardens and Overseers of the Poor of the Parish of *Groton* in the County of *Suffolk*

WE, whose Names are hereunto subscribed, being two of the *Members of the* ———— Friendly Society, called the *Benefit Club* ———— holden at the House of *Miller Cook* in the Parish of *Groton* in the County of *Suffolk* ———— established in Pursuance of the Act made in the Thirty-Third Year of his present Majesty's Reign, intituled, " An Act for the Encouragement and Relief of " Friendly Societies," do hereby certify and acknowledge, that *James Baldwin Wheelwright* Yeoman, is a Member duly admitted Into our Society as aforesaid. In Witness whereof, we have here-unto set our respective Hands and Places of Abode, the *15.* — Day of *April* in the Year of our Lord, *1795*.

Attested by
Edward Hill of the Parish of *Boxford*

Thos Le— of the Parish of *Boxford*

Robt Seonier of the Parish of *Boxford* in the County of *Suffolk* Steward of the aforesaid Society.

William his ✗ mark King of the Parish of *Boxford* Steward of the aforesaid Society.

I, *Wm. B. Brand* — one of his Majesty's Justices of the Peace, in and for the said County of *Suffolk* — — — do certify, that *Edward Hill* one of the Witnesses who attested the above-written Certificate, hath this Day made Oath before me, the said Justice, that he the said *Edward Hill* did see the above-named *Robt Seonier* and *Willm King* — whose Names are thereunto set, severally sign the said Certificate; and that the Names of *Edward Hill* and *Thos Lewis* — who are the Witnesses thereto, are respectively of their own proper Hand-writing. Given under my Hand this *15.* — — Day of *April 1795*

Wm B. Brand

Ipswich: Printed and Sold by J. BUSH, Bookseller, and Stationer. Where may be had all sorts of Blank Forms for Justices, &c.

Illustration 1. Certificate of Membership of Benefit Club, Groton (SRO, FL 50617147).

County and Trade Societies

P.H.J.H. Gosden in 1961 identified a number of friendly societies which appealed to a section of the community which was different from that attracted by either the local community based or the affiliated societies. Their constitutions resulted in very different ways of working.

COUNTY SOCIETIES

Ordinary membership participation in the affairs of a county friendly society was limited, with management of these societies resting in the hands of the honorary members. They tended to be the leading gentlemen or clergy in a county, leaving no real role for the ordinary or benefit member. Such friendly societies were, as Gosden wrote, not founded by working men, nor were they run by those they were intended to benefit.

Two sorts of record have survived from the nineteenth century as sources for information about County Societies. As with local friendly societies, the rules of many county societies have survived to be found in County Record Offices or at Kew in the PRO. These give a good idea of their aims, objectives and administration. Membership Registers form the second major type of record. Where these have been located, useful individual data have been identified as useful for extraction. The example in Illustration 2 is of the West Suffolk Society, which appears to have been formed in 1830 and in 1872 had 871 members. The typical personal data shown reveal the full name, occupation, age and home location of a member at his time of joining.

County societies had a limited geographical scope, not extending beyond the southern half of England, with a consequent relatively small combined membership.

TRADE SOCIETIES

In a different sphere, the fore-runnners of the later trade unions undertook many of the benefit provisions of friendly societies. Described in the late 18th and early 19th centuries as trade societies, they developed networks of branches for their members. Evidence has been found of their

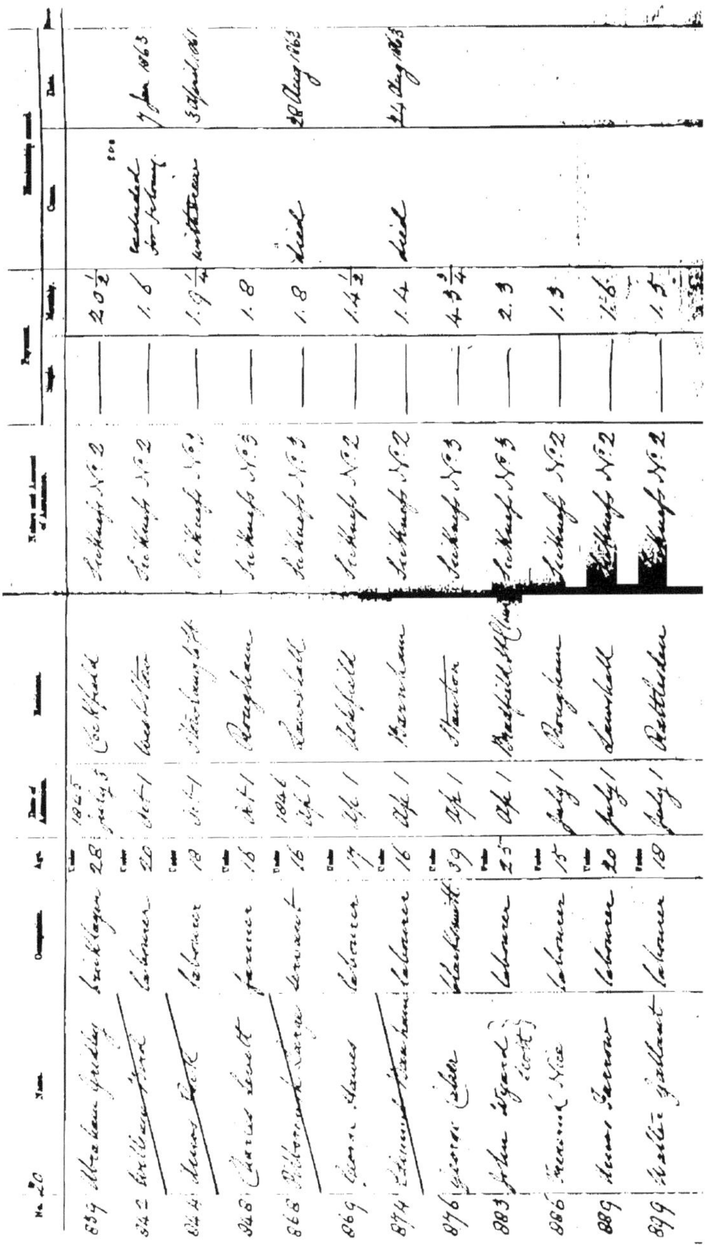

Illustration 2. Register of Members, West Suffolk FS (SRO, GF 502111).

extensive existence particularly in and around the Metropolis where such organisations were established throughout the 19th century. The commonest survival of trade societies are their rules although exceptionally other records may exist, possibly with successor organisations. As with local friendly societies the starting point for locating material will be County Record Offices and the PRO.

Affiliated Societies

MEMBERSHIP OPPORTUNITIES

The growth of the nationwide, eventually international, mutual friendly society Orders, with their own distinctive culture, raised their status and influence to undreamt of heights. Contact with Parliament through the nomination of Parliamentary Agents, involvement in Medical Aid Associations through the joint establishment of dispensaries with members of the medical profession, brought these essentially self managed working men's organisations into areas of national life never contemplated by previous generations. For individuals, opportunities unimagineable when they were young proffered themselves. With local, district or regional, and national levels of operation a man dedicated to a life of active participation in the friendly society Orders could achieve much by way of self-fulfilment, often gaining respect of thousands of his peers in the process.

Not everyone who became a subscribing member of a friendly society had the inclination or wherewithal to submerge themselves in administration. Many simply paid their contributions and drew their benefit when appropriate. Quite a few found the regular financial demands too much and dropped out, or "lapsed" as it was termed. As a consequence it is those who rose to positions of seniority, or gave valuable service in a particular branch or district or recorded lengthy spells of service, who tend have the greatest amount of personal detail recorded.

EXTENT OF RECORD SURVIVAL

On the evidence of the NRA data for friendly society Orders, the larger part of extant records relate to the big two Orders, i.e. the Ancient Order of Foresters and the Independent Order of Oddfellows (Manchester Unity). At their height they had branches almost literally from John o'Groats to Lands End. There was a multiplicity of smaller Orders, however the survival rate of their records has not been good. A list of the largest Orders functioning in 1887, together with some of the initials that research into their activities will uncover, is provided after the Glossary of Terms. The detailed study of the culture of friendly society Orders is still in its infancy and much remains to be done on developing an understanding of the full distribution of local units of the Orders, the need being for widespread local research to be undertaken to discover the rise and fall of a society's fortunes.

By no means is a full coverage of all members available for any of the Orders. The expectation of finding specific references to an individual should not be too great. It must also be made clear that although described as branches, local units of Orders were essentially autonomous and exercised control over their own books. No central authority could insist on their deposit with an archive, hence the patchiness and uncertainty about their survival. Sufficient material exists, nevertheless, to be of interest and value to family historians.

On the subject of the term "affiliated Order", David Hey, *The Oxford Companion to Local and Family History,* (OUP, 1996), makes a distinction between local societies and the affiliated societies which requires comment. Courts and Lodges of the Orders were not affiliated *to,* but were rather affiliated *in* nationwide, indeed international organisations. This is important in understanding members' perceptions of the Order of which they played both a large and a small part.

As indicated previously the largest affiliated friendly societies or Orders in the United Kingdom were the Foresters and the Oddfellows (Manchester Unity). Total membership of the two around the turn of the 19th century was above two million and for that reason, if no other, it is likely that for many family historians researching the activities of their forebears, it will be the names of those two societies which occur.

CENTRAL RECORDS

Order Directories/List of Lodges

A feature of the Orders was their capacity to collect and publish extensive information about their membership, financial value, sickness data, average ages, etc. The results are to be found in their annual publications which provide a useful base from which to start research.

From the establishment of the Ancient Order of Foresters in August 1834 efforts were made to ensure the availablity of a comprehensive record of all district and local branches. Early editions of the Foresters' Directory were unsophisticated and it was not until 1845 that they began to be consistent in content. Samuel Shawcross, Permanent Secretary of the AOF from 1843 to 1889 compiled the Order Directories annually with his son, remarking in the Notice prefacing the 1852 edition that

"the present publication is intended as a guide to those who feel an interest in the Order, and are desirous of knowing its extent, and the various localities in which it is established as well to those, who from adverse circumstances, or other causes, are compelled to travel from town to town in search of employment and who are desirous of availing themselves of the little assistance our travelling system affords."

From an early period the Oddfellows (Manchester Unity) compiled a similar central source of information about itself entitled "List of the Lodges". With early editions being rare, it is only from the 1880s that the content can be described with any certainty. As with the Foresters, which itemised it's Courts, the greater part of the List was given over to the recording of the local units, the Lodges.

The other, smaller Orders appear not to have produced annual publications, restricting themselves to combined quarterly management reports/magazines, which contained lists of newly formed local units.

Court and Lodge details

From 1845 Foresters' Directories contained names and numbers of Courts grouped by Districts, numbers of Court members, addresses of Court meeting places, listings of towns and villages where Courts were present, and information about meeting nights. At this early stage there was no personal information given about Court Officers.

This format remained until 1867 when names and addresses of Court Secretaries were included with details of Courts, a major development from the family historians perspective. The Directory for that year contained information about some 3600 Courts so that the volume of personal detail becoming available from that year is extensive. The next addition to Court data was the identification of the Court Treasurer's name, although not the address from 1876.

In principle, therefore, it is possible from knowing a Court Number, or its name, to obtain some detail of men who served as Court Secretary and Treasurer, including any changes of address over a long period, the length of service in the office and what size Court it was that was being administered. A typical Foresters Directory page is shown in Illustration 3.

SUFFOLK.

For other Courts situated in this County see *Colchester District* (Essex), containing Court 3259, Sudbury; 3673, Stoke-by-Noyland.—*London United District* (Middlesex), containing Courts 3642, Haverhill; 3621, Newmarket; 7796, Little Thurlow.—*Great Yarmouth, &c., District* (Norfolk), containing Courts 2523, Gorleston; 2675, Hopton; 3102, Duncar; 3149, Beccles.—*Lynn, &c., District* (Norfolk), containing Courts 2817, Mildenhall; 3162, Lakenheath; 3279, Cowling; 4088, Moulton.—*Swafham United District* (Norfolk), containing Court 3129, Barningham.

Beccles.

eijlm 2950 GOODWILL TO MAN (C'60), 1858, King's Head, New Market-pl., Beccles; every four weeks. *x*; Sec., *W. Harper, Smallgate House, Beccles*—Treas., T. H. Pearce

glmo Bury St. Edmunds District—A 60 (1864). *L3½*.

dhj *lm* 3641 FOUNTAIN OF FRIENDSHIP (B502), 1861, Grapes, Brent-grovel-st., Bury St. Edmunds; every two weeks, *j—r*; Sec., *J. W. Cornish, 21, Crown-st., Bury St. Edmunds*—Treas., R. Lofts

dhlm 4088 ROBIN HOOD (B376), 1863, Pickerell, High-st., Ixworth; first Tuesday, *f*; Sec., *R. H. Jeffers, Pickerell Hotel, Ixworth, nr. Bury St. Edmunds*—Treas., J. Slack

dhj *lm* 4125 ROYAL OAK (B494), 1863, Boar, High-st., Walsham-le-Willows; every four weeks, *d*; Sec., *W. Kerridge, Four Ashes, Walsham-le-Willows, nr. Bury St. Edmunds*—Treas., W. Croufoot

chlm 4306 PRIDE OF THE GREEN (B829), 1864, Bull, Hartest; first Monday, *a*; Sec., *G. Clarke, The Row, Hartest, nr. Bury St. Edmunds*—Treas., A. Game

chj *lm* 5313 ANCHOR OF HOPE (B429), 1869, Anchor, The Green, Tuddenham St. Marys; every four weeks, *b*; Sec., *D. A. Barkham, The Street, Tuddenham St. Marys, Soham*—Treas., R. J. Wright

dhj *lm* 5426 ROYAL ALBERT (B482), 1870, Bell, Rickinghall; every four weeks, *k*; Sec., *W. Humphreys, Cock Inn, Botesdale, nr. Diss*—Treas., L. Ferrer

chjlm 5470 MARQUIS OF BRISTOL (B2538), 1870, The Bull, Hargrave; first Friday, *u*; Sec., *J. Cooper, Post Office, Chevington, nr. Bury St. Edmunds*—Treas., E. Pettitt

dhj *lm* 5481 PROSPERITY (B483), 1870, Swan, The Street, Woolpit; first Tuesday, *f*; Sec., *G. Hadlow, The Street, Woolpit, nr. Bury St. Edmunds*—Treas., B. Mason

dhj *lm* 5518 BARON HARTISMERE (B2729), 1870, Six Bells, High-st., Gislingham; every four weeks, *q*; Sec., *D. Elliner, Mill-st., Gislingham, nr. Eye*—Treas., W. Ruffles

dhj *lm* 5676 VICTORIA ROYAL (B653), 1872, Foresters' Hall, High-st., Hopton; first Tuesday, *f*; Sec., *W. Mann, High-st., North Lopham, nr. Thetford*—Treas., J. B. Walton

Illustration 3. Typical Ancient Order of Foresters' 'Directory' page.

20

The Oddfellows produced a similar publication to the "Directory" called the "List of Lodges". This indicated names and numbers of a Lodge together with names and addresses of Lodge Secretaries.

District details

Whilst there was a lack of personal information in the early years relating to Foresters Courts the same was not true for Districts, with outstandingly comprehensive lists of names and addresses of District Secretaries being included from the early years. The 1852 Directory, for example, lists some 162 District Secretaries' names and addresses, many of whom served in the capacity of Relieving Officer. The names of the latter are recorded separately.

By 1881 around 300 District Secretaries' names and addresses were identified, and, in a separate listing, the names of the principal officers, District Chief Rangers, Sub Chief Rangers and Treasurers, could be found. A further addition was the names and addresses of District Trustees, of whom there were normally three in a District. The men chosen to serve in this capacity were often long serving members who had made a significant contribution to the District by having occupied responsible posts.

In the Oddfellows (Manchester Unity) Lists, the names and addresses of both Corresponding Secretary and the principal officer of the district, the Provincial Grand Master, were given with Lodge detail. These were supplemented by names and addresses of both Examining and Relieving Officers of Travellers, together occasionally with their occupations.

Widows and Orphans Societies

Widows and Orphans Societies or Funds, were formed by both Foresters and Oddfellows for the purpose of supplementing the basic Funeral Allowance paid to the widows of deceased members. From 1874 Foresters Directories included Secretaries' names and addresses. The full list of these for 1881 amounted to 100 names, responsible for some 40,807 members and £53,143 in funds. (See below for details of Widows and Orphans Funds in practice).

Juvenile Societies

Juvenile Societies developed during the 19th century to become a major plank in the Friendly Society movement. The first links with the Foresters occurred in the 1840s. Individual Courts formed independent juvenile societies. Eventually in 1883 a Federation was formed which grew in both size and influence, with the High Chief Ranger for the year normally occupying the post of President. After 1896 membership of friendly societies was extended to children as young as one year.

The Foresters Directory for 1890 revealed that there were 1436 juvenile societies, with 85,125 members, a figure which, by 1900, had grown to 125,274. Names and addresses of juvenile society Secretaries are listed in the Directory; many were also Court Secretaries. Equivalent lists were recorded by the Oddfellows (MU). These show that by 1902 the Oddfellows had 1662 juvenile societies with 111,512 members.

Medical Aid Associations

A further area of activity was the Friendly Society Medical Association. These developed from around 1870, providing members who already belonged to Friendly Society branches with increased access to treatment and medicines. Details of their dispensary or institutional addresses and the names and addresses of their Secretaries and Medical Officers were included in the Foresters' Directory from 1874.

Biographies of prominent members

At the very end of the 19th century potted biographies of the men who served on the Foresters' Executive Council of the Order began to appear in Directories along with individual portrait photographs. Similar photographs also started to appear on the Oddfellows' Lists. The international development of the Foresters at this time is reflected by information concerning the Order as it existed in America, Canada and elsewhere, again with photographs of the members of the Subsidiary (overseas) Executive Councils.

Whilst the Oddfellows' Lists did not contain detailed biographies, they did schedule the names and districts of members whose portraits were published in the Oddfellows Magazine between December 1835 and April 1847, when the feature was discontinued. A continuous series of portraits was recommenced in January 1857. Of exceptional interest is the identification of dates of death, even burial locations (Illustration 4).

LIST OF PORTRAITS PUBLISHED BY THE BOARD OF DIRECTORS IN THE MAGAZINE—continued.

NO. OF MAGA- ZINE	NAME AND DISTRICT.	MAGAZINE.	BORN.	DIED.	REMARKS, WHERE BURIED, ETC.
37	John Bradley, Hyde, G.M. 1850	April, 1845	May 5, 1810	June 21, 1856	Hyde Chapel, Gee Cross.
38	Henry Whaite, Manchester, G.M. 1844	July, "	Aug. 20, 1803	July 26, 1869	Brooklands Cemetery, Manchester.
39	Joseph Woodcock, Glossop, G.M. 1862	Oct., "	Oct. 13, 1803	Nov. 1, 1870	Independent Chapel, Glossop.
40	Henry Ratcliffe, 'C.S. of the Order,' Chowbent	Jan., 1846	Nov. 4, 1808	May 25, 1877	Brooklands Cemetery, Manchester, June 2; Mont. by the [Order.
41	William Candelett, Hyde	April, "	Dec. 17, 1802	Mar. 9, 1867	Died in London.
42	John Dickenson, Manchester, G.M. 1845	July, "		1811	Parish Church, Burslem, February 23.
43	Robert Glass, Potteries, G.M. 1852	Oct., "		Feb. 20, 1881	Died at the Isle of Man.
44	John B. Rogerson, Manchester	Jan., 1847	Jan. 20, 1809	Oct. 15, 1859	G.N. Cemetery, Southgate; Mon. by N. London District.
45	James Roe, North London, G.M. 1859	April, "	Oct. 18, 1805	Nov. 24, 1861	

After this date the Portraits were discontinued in the Magazine, which lingered until July, 1848, when the publication ceased; re-issued Jan. 1857.

NO. OF MAGA- ZINE	NAME AND DISTRICT.	MAGAZINE.	BORN.	DIED.	REMARKS, WHERE BURIED, ETC.
1	John Schofield, Bradford, G.M. 1855	Jan., 1857	Jan. 21, 1810	June 10, 1890	Undercliffe Cemetery, Bradford
2	James C. Cox, Southampton, G.M. 1855	April, "	Aug. 30, 1818		
3	William Aitken, Ashton-under-Lyne	July, "	Dec., 1814	Sept. 27, 1869	Burial Ground of St. Peter's Church.
4	Samuel Daynes, Norwich, G.M. 1851	Oct., "	Dec. 16, 1815	June 12, 1890	The Rosary, Norwich
5	B.G. Davies, Merthyr Tydvil	Jan., 1858	Nov. 4, 1822		
6	Charles Hardwick, Preston, G.M. 1857	April, "	Sept. 10, 1817	July 8, 1889	Brooklands Cemetery, Manchester.
7	Benjamin Street, Wirksworth, G.M. 1854	July, "	April 8, 1803	Jan. 6, 1888	Wirksworth Cemetery.
8	Henry Buck, Birmingham, G.M. 1860	Oct., "	July 12, 1813	Jan. 22, 1876	The Cemetery, Warton Lane, Birmingham.
9	John Gale, Liverpool, G.M. 1861	Jan., 1859	1818	Oct. 26, 1808	St. James's Cemetery, October 29.
10	Dr. Thomas Price, Aberdare, G.M. 1865	April, "	April 1, 1822	Feb. 29, 1888	Calvaria Chapel, Aberdare.
11	Frederick Richmond, Manchester, G.M. 1864	July, "	Dec. 17, 1799	April 15, 1888	Ardwick Cemetery, Manchester.
12	James S. Banyard, Bury St. Edmunds	Jan., "	Mar. 23, 1816	Aug. 27, 1887	
13	Augustus F.A. Greaves, Victoria, Australia	April, "	1865	May 23, 1874	Melbourne, Australia.
14	William Hickton, Stockport, G.M. 1859	July, "	Feb. 24, 1823	Mar. 14, 1880	Stockport Cemetery.
15	James Webb, Hyde	July, "	June 10, 1808	July 17, 1868	St. George's Church, Hyde; Monument by Hyde District.
16	James Reynolds, Cowbridge	Oct., "	Mar. 24, 1792	Nov. 25, 1872	
17	John Richardson, Cockermouth, G.M. 1848	April, 1861	July 26, 1816		
18	Bryant Allen, Norwich	April, "	Oct. 23, 1806	Sept. 12, 1870	Rosary Cemetery, September 19.
19	Henry Williams, Shrewsbury	July, "	1820		
20	Thomas Kilner, Eccles	Oct., "	1808	Mar. 12, 1863	Eccles Parish Church, March 15.
21	Samuel Taylor Settle, Bolton	Jan., 1862	July 13, 1811		
22	William B. Smith, Birmingham, G.M. 1947	April, "	Sept. , 1821	Mar. 24, 1895	
23	Vincent R. Burgess, South London, G.M. 1863	July, "	Feb. 11, 1815	Mar. 17, 1870	Woking Cemetery.
24	Andrew Rourke, Liverpool	Oct., "	May 20, 1810	April 29, 1874	
25	Thomas Loaf, Liverpool, G.M. 1849	Jan., 1863	July 24, 1813	May 22, 1869	Died in New York.
26	Edwin Noon, Belper	April, "	Aug. 21, 1820	May, 1868	
27	William N. Waldram, Leicester	July, "	July 29, 1814	Sept. 9, 1881	Leicester Cemetery, September 7.

Illustration 4. Typical Independent Order of Oddfellows (MU) 'List of Lodges' page.

Summary

Foresters' Directories and the Oddfellows' (Manchester Unity) Lists provide unrivalled sources of detailed information about those who played a significant part in the administration of the Order at national, district and local level. However, no indexing of this data in a form suitable for ready use by family historians yet exists. Consequently identification of a specific name requires the investment of a substantial amount of time. A further obstacle to ready retrieval of names is the scarcity of the publications themselves. A complete set of Foresters' Directories exists in the collection of the Foresters' Heritage Trust. The Oddfellows' (Manchester Unity) Lists appear to be less complete, nevertheless some District Offices are known to hold reasonably substantial runs from the late 1880s onwards.

Journals and magazines

A useful source giving an insight into the activities of the membership of the Orders is the monthly/quarterly publication associated with a particular Order. The titles of some of these are given at the end of this booklet. Survival of anything like complete sets is the exception rather than the rule. If available, their contents can be enormously illuminating for the family historian as the topics listed below show.

Illustrated biographies

By the early 1840s the Orders were maturing into acceptable, although still illegal, societies. Men of strong character and substantial ability were joining not simply for the benefits but for the increasingly significant social cachet attached to membership. Astonishingly details of their efforts were recorded by contemporaries and form the basis for much of the detailed occupational/class analysis that has been undertaken. In the Foresters, as each year the administration moved from town to town, a new group of eight men was chosen to be the Executive Committee of the Order and of these one, considered by his peers to be the most able, was selected as High Chief Ranger. It was these outstanding members who had their achievements, their tastes, their concerns eloquently recorded for posterity and their likenesses recorded in this pre-photographic age by an engraved line portrait. Unwittingly an important archive about working men whose lives are unlikely to have otherwise featured in any historical documentation was assembled, in the *Foresters' 'Miscellany'*.

Changes in proprietorship, editors and policy meant the discontinuation of such rich material from the late 1840s until 1861 when the practice of featuring a deserving member recommenced. With greater numbers of members being featured it was no longer simply the High Chief Ranger for the year who was revealed to the world but members who had played a significant part at Court or District levels of the Order. A complete list of the names of members honoured in this way is available for the period up to 1914 and an example of the format of an illustrated biography is depicted in Illustrations 5 and 6.

Both Oddfellows' and Ancient Druids' magazines contained detailed biographical accounts of members in what were named Portraits. As mentioned above, full listings of Oddfellows honoured in this way are contained in their 'Lists of Lodges'.

Illustration 5. Foresters' portrait.

25

The Foresters' Review.

EDMUND ASHWORTH, P.H.C.R.

[WITH A PORTRAIT.]

In a brief memoir of those whose portraits are from time to time selected to appear in the *Miscellany*, it does not always follow as a natural consequence that we should faithfully chronicle every incident in their private lives and character ; and when, as in the case of Br. Edmund Ashworth, the subject of our present sketch, their lives have been so unostentatious, their character so unpretending, so unattended with all those striking circumstances which mark the lives of heroes and statesmen, about all that is required in these pages is his parentage, birth, and marriage. But in his character as a Forester, which is with what we more chiefly have to do, he has attained a high position in the Order, and has fairly and honourably earned the title to be placed amongst our eminent men in that niche which the collective wisdom of the society has provided for this purpose, and to have his name handed down to posterity as one of the early fathers, if not pioneers, of our institution.

The parents of Br. Ashworth resided at Edenfield, in the county of Lancaster, and followed the industrious calling of flannel weavers, the staple trade of the district, and there on the 20th April, 1818, our brother was born. By frugality and care his parents contrived to give him a better education than fell to the lot of most of the sons of toil in Lancashire at this particular time. When he was about four years of age, his parents removed with him to Spotland Bridge, near Rochdale, of which neighbourhood they were natives. At about twelve years of age their son was put to work in the warehouse of a cotton mill as a maker-up of twist, and afterwards was taught the calling of a cotton warper at the same place. This occupation he continued to follow for a number of years. In 1836, Br. Ashworth married Rhoda, daughter of Mr. Samuel Harrison, a native of Shelf, Yorkshire, but at that time residing in Rochdale, and in the employment of Messrs. Petrie, engineers and ironfounders, where he remained nearly forty years—a fact which speaks well for his character. The fruits of this marriage were nine children, seven of whom are still living.

In a short time after his marriage Br. Ashworth became connected with our Order, being initiated in Court No. 85, on the 11th February, 1837. On the same night he was elected secretary of the Court, and retained the office until he was appointed to the more important one in the District. In July, 1839, a vacancy occurred in the office of D.S. of the Rochdale Town District, and Br. Ashworth was selected to fill it. At the following October meeting he was again elected D.S., and at each subsequent election up to this time has been re-elected, and therefore must have been faithful to the trust reposed in him.

There are few amongst our leading brethren who have been in the Order so long as Br. Ashworth, but who, in the progressive changes which have taken

Illustration 6. Foresters' potted biography.

Births, marriages and deaths

Whilst the recording of the vital events in an individual's life is something which can be tackled from other sources (eg. *An Introduction to Civil Registration,* Tom Wood, Federation of Family History Societies, 1994) a birth, death or marriage notice in the context of a friendly society provides an added dimension to the information. Early editions of an Order's magazines contained detail of this human dimension. The following two examples come from *The Ancient Foresters Miscellany.*

"April 1st, 1844, at six o'clock in the morning, Christiana, wife of Br. James Wilson, S. W W, of Court St Helen, No 1048, Auckland, of a son and daughter, who, with the mother are doing well. And at four 'clock the same afternoon. Mary, daughter of the above James and Christiana Wilson, died, aged two years and six months."

"May 12th (1844) at the parish church of Ashton-under-Lyne, by the Rev. John Handsforth, Br. John Bacon, P.C. and P.S., also P.A.P. and P.S. of Court No. 5, to Miss Mary Higginbotham, fourth daughter of Joseph Higginbotham of Charles Town, in the parish of Glossop."

Management reports

A fundamental feature of the Foresters, Oddfellows (Manchester Unity) and other Orders was the regular report by the managing body to members. Whilst this dealt primarily with the 'business' activities they occasionally contained information about individuals of interest to the family historian.

The Executive Council of the Foresters produced a Quarterly Report to all Courts, disseminating administrative and legal information, financial accounts and, of particular value to family historians, listings of delegates from Courts and Districts to the Annual High Court Meeting. Each year several hundred members came together from all over Great Britain to contribute to a week's debates about the formulation of new General Laws and other business matters. From the annual listings, the number of years and the regularity of attendance by a particular Court member can be identified, whilst personal achievement in the Order, for example Court Secretary, or District Chief Ranger is indicated with the delegates name.

Quarterly Reports produced by the Oddfellows (Manchester Unity) contained only administrative material with little appertaining to individuals. The combined Quarterly Reports/Magazines of Orders such as the United Ancient Order of Druids or the British United Oddfellows fused together the features found in the separate publications of the Foresters and Oddfellows (Manchester Unity), containing both business material and biographies of members.

DISTRICT RECORDS

The intermediate level of operation of the Orders was at what was normally termed the District level. The exact composition of this varied from Order to Order. To the Manchester Unity, it was a geographically based unit, composed of the local branches (Lodges) within defined boundaries. For the Foresters' a District was less structured being simply a confederation of two or more branches (Courts) which agreed to act together for certain benefits, primarily the operation of a burial fund. These might cross local and even County boundaries, or be co-terminus with other Courts in the same vicinity belonging to a different district.

Reports
Within both Orders districts proliferated. Foresters' Districts in England peaked at 218 in 1880, in Scotland the maximum of 20 districts was attained in 1884, this level being sustained for the next 25 years. Wales greatest number was 26 in 1894. With over 250 districts thus extant at one time or another it might be hoped that a high percentage of their meeting reports would have survived. In the event, a figure of 5% might be realistic.

Committee membership listings
Each Foresters' District was run by a Committee of Management, comprising elected officers. These were chosen from Court members with sufficient time and interest in the work of the Order who served for a year, organising regular District business meetings, administering the Rules, arranging fund-raising social events, etc.

The Rochester and Medway District was formed in 1861 from four Courts meeting in Chatham, Cliffe and Rochester. Recorded in their printed Reports which contained a variety of detail about the work and activities of the District are the names of the men who took office over the following years. Periodically, the posts were subject to election, thus by following through the consecutive Reports a substantive list of all the main office holders, with their respective Court numbers, can be compiled. The latter is important since the Court meeting place will be a good guide, at least until well towards the end of the century, of the home location of a member. The following is how, typically, the available information can be used.

District Chief Ranger	District Sub Chief Ranger	District Secretary	District Treasurer
Edwin G Frid (2644)	John Evenden (3128)	Henry Platts (1713)	James Dark (2644)
Henry Kybett (1713)	John Evenden (3128)	Henry Platts (1713)	James Dark (2644)
Wm Tillman(1713)	John Melton (1713)		
John Evenden (3128)	Thomas Huggett (3128)		James Dark (2644)
Thomas Huggett (3128)	J. Roberts (1713)		
F.(?) Huggett (3128)			— Gallon (3475)
J Roberts (1713)	S. Boreman(2644)		A. Brown (2644)

The meeting places of Courts mentioned and their members home towns were, therefore:

3475	Brompton	— Gallon
1713	Chatham	Henry Platts, Henry Kybett, Wm Tillman, John Melton, J. Roberts
3128	Chatham	Thomas Huggett, F. (?) Huggett, John Evendon
2644	Rochester	Edwin G. Frid, James Dark(e), S. Boreman, A. Brown

Court delegates to District Meetings

District meetings comprised delegates elected from Courts to attend and speak on issues of interest to a Court. The names and Court numbers were always recorded in the Quarterly Reports and from these a good chronological listing of an individual involvement can be demonstrated.

The South London District was founded in 1846 and from its records the sometimes astonishing commitment of Court members to District matters is evident. Whilst many did their duty by attending once or twice as delegates others built up attendance records spread over 30, 40, even approaching 50 years . One such member was Bro. John Fisher of Court "Star of Surrey", No. 1392 (Newington Butts). His first attendance was in July 1851 and his last, July 1899. Bro. Fisher was for much of this period Court Secretary, and in addition held office in his local lodge and District of Oddfellows. Courts had differing ways of selecting their delegate, some choosing the Secretary, thus ensuring continuity others rewarding the Chief Ranger for the time being by sending him.

Funeral Fund payments

The principal financial objective of Foresters' Districts was to establish a fund from which funeral payments could be made to widows of members, and to members on the death of their wives. Contained within District Reports are the accounts of such funds, and usually listed are the names of the deceased member or the member's name where it is the wife who died. Some Districts included Mortality Lists in which were recorded dates of death or dates when payment of benefit was made, sometimes with the age at death being shown, sometimes the cause of death. The content and quality of such information varied both geographically and in time, with older district records being less informative than later ones.

From the Foresters' Rochester and Medway District Quarterly Reports the identification of the following names serves to illustrate how individuals can be pinpointed. The list is compiled by associating information in the Accounts with a separate membership report in which the full names of deceased members and their Court numbers are shown.

Quarterly Meeting date	Members name	Court No.	Location
16/7/1861	Thomas M. Jones	1713	Chatham.
	H. Broad (for wife)	–	
10/10/1861	S. J. Hastrick	3089	New Brompton
	Walter Underwood	2644	Rochester
	James Bartholomew	3601	Chatham
9/1/1862	W. Mills	2644	Rochester
10/4/1862	– Lambert (for wife)	2644	Rochester
	C. Bradley	2644	Rochester
10/7/1862	– Bailey	3089	New Brompton
	J. Hick (for wife)	3089	New Brompton
	Andrews (for wife)	1713	Chatham
9/10/1862	J. Young	1713	Chatham
	C. Kettle	1713	Chatham

Widows and Orphans Fund

Supplementing the Funeral Fund in many Foresters' Districts was a voluntary Widows and Orphans Fund. Contributions to this fund, which paid out allowances to a deceased Brother's wife and children, were optional and consequently the balances in them did not grow to large amounts as could be found in a Funeral Fund. The amounts in the two Funds in Rochester and Medway District, for example, demonstrate this. In brackets are the numbers of contributing members.

Date	Funeral Fund				Widows and Orphans Fund			
	£	s	d		£	s	d	
January 1862	87	5	7	(735)	38	11	4	
January 1867	844	4	1	(2767)	83	13	3	(18)
January 1872	2106	3	7	(3186)	125	16	0	(35)

The smaller scale of operation of the Widows and Orphans Fund in the Medway area meant that although the occasional payment is recorded to a widow, whose name is given, and the number of children being supported, there is little scope for it to be useful for family historians. Of far greater value is information available in the District Minutes of the South London District (SLD), comprised of Courts mostly meeting in metropolitan Kent, Surrey and Middlesex. Here a fund of sizeable proportions was established; however, as it turned out, at the eventual cost of the demands of the numbers of beneficiaries far outstripping the income.

By way of comparison between the two Districts, the following table gives information relating to the SLD on the same basis as for Rochester and Medway.

Date	Funeral Fund				Widows and Orphans Fund			
	£	s	d		£	s	d	
January 1862	2559	2	5	(3500)	4465	18	8	(3228)
January 1867	4908	17	3	(4836)	8932	11	3	(4597)
January 1872	6748	9	1	(5424)	12313	12	9	(5402)

With over 5000 contributing members clearly the number of beneficiaries would, as members grew old and died, become significant. By January 1872, the number of SLD Courts with members benefitting was 45, and the number of families (that is widows and/or orphans) receiving payment from the Widows and Orphans Fund 219. Listings of recipients of money from the Widows and Orphans Funds were included in the accounts section of the District's Quarterly Reports. The distribution of such Funds across the the country was patchy; by no means all counties had such an arrangement.

COURT AND LODGE RECORDS

Minute Books

At their greatest scale of operation Foresters' Courts and Oddfellows' Lodges could be found in most towns and villages of any reasonable size throughout Great Britain. The table below shows the years of the greatest extent of the Foresters.

	Year	No. of Courts
England	1893	3614
Scotland	1901	230
Wales	1894	300

As with District reports, however, the survival rate of Court/Lodge Minute Books has been extremely low. There was no requirement that they should be kept for any specified period of time so in many ways the survival of what does remain is fortuitous. Those that do survive are usually in manuscript and hard to decipher.

Officers' listings

Regularly, either at 6 or 12 monthly intervals, the officer posts in a Foresters' Court needed to be filled by election. Whilst it became the practice for a Secretary and often a Treasurer to serve for more than one year, the Chief Ranger (Chairman) and remaining five posts were often the object of much competition. Court Minutes normally show the outcomes of these annual elections from which lists of a Court's officers over a period of time can be reconstructed.

Elections for the Oddfellows officers were regulated along similar lines, and with a run of consecutive Minute Books, the names of those holding office can be tracked.

Members attending meetings

Minutes sometimes but not always began with a record being made of the names of those members attending a particular meeting. Where this evidence is available the active, as opposed to passive, membership of an individual can be identified.

Sickness and Mortality lists

A regular item of Court and Lodge business was a report on Members who were "on the funds" and of those who had died since the previous meeting. The sickness list is of particular interest in revealing a particular detail about an individual which is unlikely to be noted elsewhere. The example illustrated relates to a meeting of Foresters' Court "Egerton and Wyndham" No. 3260, held at Rustington, Sussex on Monday 13th June 1881 (Illustration 7).

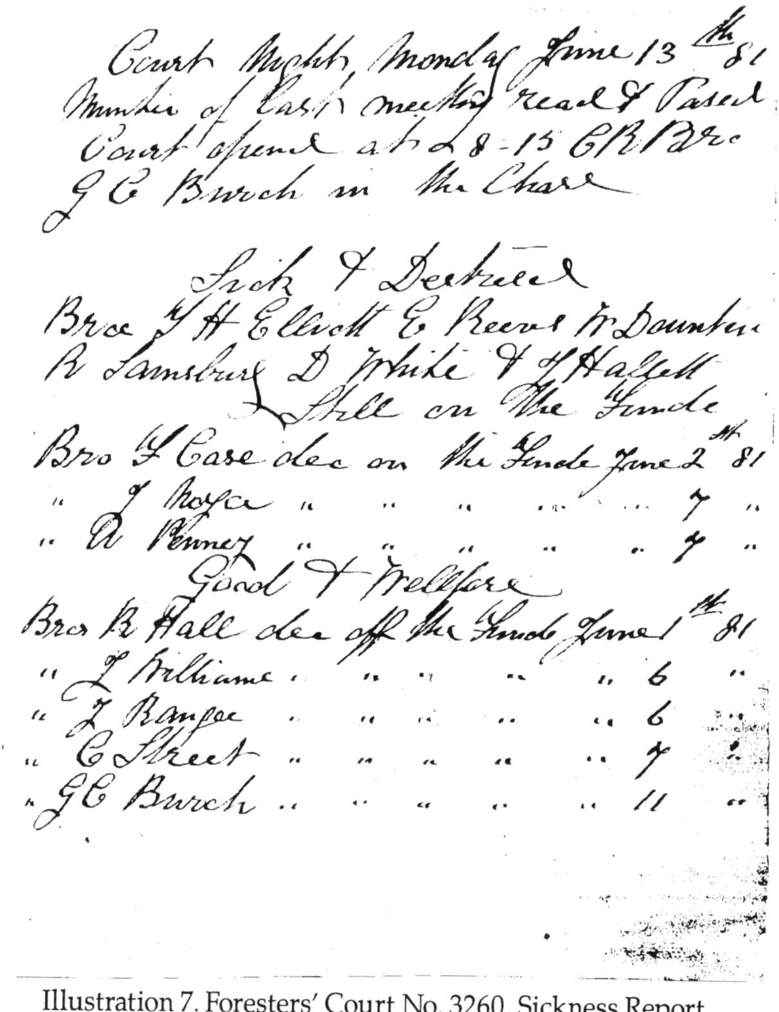

Court Night, Monday June 13th 81
Minutes of Last meeting read & Passed
Court opened at 8-15 C R Bro
J G Burch in the Chair

Sick & Destressed
Bro J H Elliott E Reeves W Dounten
R Sainsbury D White & J Hallett
Still on the Funds
Bro J Case dec on the Funds June 2nd 81
" J Royce " " " " " 7 "
" A Penney " " " " " 7 "
Good & Wellfare
Bro R Hall dec off the Funds June 1st 81
" J Williams " " " " " 6 "
" J Rampe " " " " " 6 "
" C Street " " " " " 7 "
" J G Burch " " " " " 11 "

Illustration 7. Foresters' Court No. 3260, Sickness Report.

Proposition Books

One of the most useful sources for personal detail of those who joined the Orders comes from Proposition Books. In these are listed the name, address, date of joining, age and marital status of an individual. In addition the name of the person proposing and seconding the admission of the individual is also given.

Membership Registers

Very few original membership registers survive since periodically, perhaps when a new Secretary took up post, perhaps when the information about a new member was amended, they were rewritten. Nevertheless those which do exist can be helpful in recording members joining a Court or Lodge over a period of time, with detail such as age, occupation and marital status.

Sickness Registers

With the provision of financial support being the prime objective records of those receiving benefit and the period over which it was paid were essential to the efficient management of a Court or Lodges' Accounts. Early evidence as to the form such records took is rare, however later in the 19th century, regularly formatted ledgers were produced, and were used by the Orders.

Funeral Money Books (Nominations)

The key to the correct operation of payment of any monies due at the death of a member was an unchallengeable document identifying any beneficiary. This was achieved by means of a Funeral Money Book, which took the form of individual nomination sheets in a bound book. A dated nomination form (see Illustration 8) identified the member making provision for the allocation of his money, the name of the nominee and his home town, and the name of a witness to the signing of the form.

INDIVIDUAL RECORDS

Membership Cards

On joining the Foresters an individual would be provided with a small booklet which contained the Rules of the Court of which he was a member and pages used for noting contributions paid. At the front was a 'Certificate of Membership' prefaced by the instruction that

*The Wife, Father, Mother, Child, Brother or Sister, Nephew or Niece of the Member.—Section 31 of 18 and 19 Vic., c. 63.

Ancient Order of Foresters' Friendly Society,

Registered Pursuant to Act of Parliament.

Court _Bauli of the Source_ No. 3273

March 23 1863

I HEREBY nominate* _My Son John Mullins_

of _Bristol_ in the County of _Gloucester_ to receive

the Money payable at my Death by the Court above-named.

Arthur Breene Witness. _Charles Mullins_ his + mark Signature.

I HEREBY revoke the above nomination _Charles Mullins_ his + mark Signature.

H. Poole Witness. _May 11_ 1868

Illustration 8. Foresters' Court No. 3273, Death Benefit nomination form.

"When a member receives a Copy of these Rules, he is to read them attentively. He will not be allowed to plead ignorance should he act contrary to them. The whole will be strictly enforced."

From the contributions record pages shown in Illustration 9 something of the nature of the friendly societies organisation can be deduced. George Harris, a member of Court "Unity", No. 5340 meeting at the Star Inn in Burnham, Essex was, according to his membership booklet, initiated on the 18th February 1874. At his first meeting he paid an entrance fee of 15/- (75p) which was received by Thomas Ambrose, the Court Secretary. Comparison of the level of fee with the table of contributions and benefits reveals that Brother Harris was 29 years old at the time of joining. For the monthly contribution of 2/3d (12p), Harris was entitled to receive the full benefits of 14 shillings (70p) weekly sick pay for 26 weeks, followed by 7 shillings (35p) for the next 26 weeks after which for the remainder of the sickness, 5 shillings (25p). A death benefit of £12 for the member, £6 for the member's wife was included. For a further payment of 1s 6d (17p) to the Doctor's Fund, he was entitled to receive "medicines and attendance" when sick. It can also be seen that Brother Harris did not subscribe to the Widows and Orphans Fund.

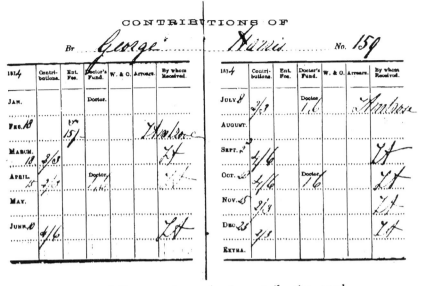

Illustration 9. Foresters' member's contribution card.

Personal Membership documents of the type illustrated are not common, but if they are encountered amongst family papers they can prove hugely informative.

Membership/Past Chief Ranger's Certificates

One of the more artistic items likely to be of interest to family historians is the decorative Membership or Past Officer's Certificate. Not only do they bear the names of an individual but they contain names of the principal Court/Lodge Officers together with Court/Lodge Number, making identification of the home location relatively straightforward.

Membership Certificates were available from the commencement of the Ancient Order of Foresters in 1834, evolving over the years into highly attractive documents worthy of being placed in walnut frames and hung in parlours. Past District Chief Ranger and Past Provincial Grand Master Certificates recorded the year of achievment of an individual who had served as a District chairman.

Unlike the majority of records described in this Introduction, Certificates are as likely to be found in second hand shops as in recognised documentary archives.

Medals/Jewels

The tradition of awarding medals, or what later became known as jewels, to members was common to all friendly society Orders. They were presented to those who performed valuable services to an Order by serving as a Branch or District Officer. Often, and this is how they are of use to family historians, they were engraved on the obverse side with the name of the recipient and reason for the award.

Other Records

NEWSPAPERS

As a source of information about the activities of individuals who actively participated in the work of friendly societies, newspapers can be rewarding. Whilst few reports were made of regular business meetings, creating a misleading sense of inactivity, annual or celebratory dinners regularly were covered by the press.

In September 1877 a dinner and presentation were given to James Joshua Holmes, a man who had started life in the vicinity of Borough High Street where he had entered the family hairdressing business. Eventually he was to mix with M.P.s at the House of Commons where he performed the duties of Parliamentary Agent for the Manchester Unity of Oddfellows. The celebratory occasion marked his election to the highest post in the MU, that of Grand Master of the Order.

The South London Press report of the occasion was extensive, listing the names of national and local dignatories who attended the function, as well as describing Bro Holmes' Friendly Society activities over 34 years during which he had devotedly served both Oddfellows and Foresters.

DIARIES

Amongst the most elusive records which would show what involvement with Friendly Societies meant to an individual are diaries. Whilst friendly societies are mentioned in well known diaries, such as that of Francis Kilvert, and, very briefly, in those of some working men, a really revealing record of the thoughts of an active member is sadly lacking.

HONOURS BOARDS

Many Courts and Lodges furnished their meeting rooms in public houses and other venues with Honours Boards. On these were recorded the names of (usually) the principal officers of the branch. The more elaborate of these boards often took the form of a triptych with the names of the officers on the two wings and the Court or Lodge Dispensation in a gilded frame in the centre portion. Local museums may have these on display, although given their size, they may well be in store, awaiting availability of adequate space for their suitable presentation.

Glossary of Terms

A Friendly Society **'Order'** had local units best described as branches, which had a large degree of autonomy in defining their own contributions and benefits but which nevertheless only existed by the express authority of a central administrative body.

Members of Affiliated Societies were called **"Brothers"** and **"Sisters"** in recognition of the fraternal nature of the friendly society movement. Whilst there was rivalry there was little competitiveness between the various Orders, and many individuals were members of more than one Order.

A **"Dispensation"** was the formal document, some 27 inches (68 cm) by 20 inches (51cm) which was the legal authority issued by the Executive Council of the Ancient Order of Foresters to the founder members of a new Court. The Dispensation bore the Arms of the Order, the name and meeting place of the new Court, the names of the three founder members and the names of the eight members of the Executive Council. It was dated and bore the embossed seal of the Order. Similar documents were issued by the Manchester Unity.

Prominent Friendly Society Orders

Names; Foundation dates; Abbreviated names; Administrative body; Annual meeting description; Officers titles and initials

Ancient Order of Foresters Friendly Society [1834](AOF)
Executive Council. (EC) Annually elected national committee.
Elected at annual moveable delegate conference
High Court' [HCM].

HCR	High Chief Ranger	National Chairman EC
HSCR	High Sub Chief Ranger	National Vice Chairman EC
HCT	High Court Treasurer	Member EC
HCS	High Court Secretary	Member EC
HCSW	High Court Senior Woodward	Member EC
HCJW	High Court Junior Woodward	Member EC
HCSB	High Court Senior Beadle	Member EC
HCJB	High Court Junior Beadle	Member EC
PS	Permanent Secretary	
	Trustee	

The above Officers titles were in use from 1834 to 1911

DCR	District Chief Ranger	District Chairman
DSCR	District Sub Chief Ranger	District Vice Chairman
DT	District Treasurer	
DS	District Secretary	
	Trustee	
CR	Chief Ranger	Branch [Court] Chairman
SCR	Sub Chief Ranger	Branch Vice Chairman
SWW	Senior Woodward	
JWW	Junior Woodward	
SB	Senior Beadle	
JB	Junior Beadle	
	Trustee	

Independent Order of Oddfellows, Manchester Unity [1813] (IOOF(MU))

Board of Directors
Elected at Annual Movable Committee [AMC] to 1904
From 1904 Annual Movable Conference

GM	Grand Master	National Chairman
DGM	Deputy Grand Master	National Vice Chairman
	Director	Member, Board
CS	Corresponding Secretary	
PGM	Provincial Grand Master	District Chairman
PDGM	Provincial Deputy Grand Master	District Vice Chairman
Prov.CS	Provincial Corresponding Secretary	District Secretary
NG	Noble Grand	Branch [Lodge] Chairman
VG	Vice Grand	Branch Vice Chairman

Loyal Order of Ancient Shepherds, Ashton Unity [1826] (LOAS(AU))

Board of Management
Elected at Annual Moveable Conference [AMC1

CS	Chief Shepherd	National Chairman
DCS	Deputy Chief Shepherd	National Vice Chairman
CS	Corresponding Secretary	
DPCS	District Provincial Chief Shepherd	District Chairman
WM	Worthy Master	Branch [Lodge] Chairman

National United Order of Free Gardeners [1820]

Elected at Annual General Meeting

GM	Grand Master	National Chairman
DGM	Deputy Grand Master	National Vice Chairman
GS	Grand Secretary	
GT	Grand Treasurer	
DM	District Master	District Chairman
DT	District Treasurer	

42

Friendly Society Orders in existence 1887 not listed above

Ancient Order of Romans
Ancient Order of Shepherds [Second degree of AOF until 1888]
Independent Order of Rechabites
Order of the Sons of Temperance Order of Druids
Ancient Noble Order of Oddfellows
Bolton Unity British United Order of Oddfellows
Grand United Order of Oddfellows
Kingston Unity of Oddfellows
National Independent Order of Oddfellows
Nottingham Imperial Order of Oddfellows

Friendly Society Orders journals and magazines

The Foresters 'Miscellany'
The Oddfellows Magazine IOOF (MU)
The Shepherds Magazine LOAS (AU)
The Rechabite Magazine
The National United Free Gardeners Magazine
The Magazine of the Grand United Order of Oddfellows
The Order of Druids Journal
The Son of Temperance

Selective Further Reading

The Friendly Societies in England, 1815-1875 by P.H.J.H. Gosden is currently still the basic account for getting to know about FS, especially the Orders.

Mutual Aid in the Victorian Countryside, 1830-1914 by David Neave provides a detailed insight into the activities of friendly societies in the East Riding of Yorkshire.

By the Members, For the Members and *Grandfather was in the Ancient Order of Foresters* by Audrey Fisk, two pamphlets drawing on material held by the Foresters Heritage Trust which develop themes relating to membership of the AOF.

High Court Meetings of the Ancient Order of Foresters, 1835-1995 by Roger Logan presents an illustrated account of the various features of the annual AOF delegate conference.

The last three booklets mentioned can be obtained from the Foresters Heritage Trust (FHT), as can an Index to material deposited with the Trust. Enquiries should be made to FHT, Ancient Order of Foresters, College Place, Southampton, SO15 2FE

A useful contact for further information about current research into friendly societies activities during the 19th and 20th centuries is:

The Friendly Societies Research Group
c/o The Open University
Gardiner 2
Walton Hall
Milton Keynes
MK7 6AA

The author gratefully acknowledges the permission granted by the Executive Council of the Ancient Order of Foresters to quote from material held by the Foresters Heritage Trust.

APPENDIX A
English Friendly Society Records

	Local/ County FS	AOF	ODDFELLOWS (type)		OTHER ORDERS		TOTAL
BEDFORDSHIRE	9	2	16	IOOF (MU)	2	(NatFrGdnrs)	29
BERKSHIRE	11	6	0		0		17
BUCKINGHAMSHIRE	4	4	1	IOOF(MU)	0		9
CAMBRIDGESHIRE	11	10	4	IOOF (MU)	2	(LOAS)(AU)	30
					3	(LOAS)(W11)	
CHESHIRE	14	2	1	GUOOF	1	(SonsTemp)	22
					4	IOOF (MU)	
CORNWALL	7	18	7	IOOF(MU)	0		32
CUMBERLAND	6	0	5	IOOF(MU)	0		11
DERBYSHIRE	33	2	5	IOOF (MU)	2	(LOAS)(AU)	43
					1	(SonsTemp)	
DEVON	13	23	0		1	(AoDruids)	37
DORSET	6	3	1	IOOF (MU)	0		10
DURHAM	8	1	2	IOOF (MU)		(Gtemplars)	14
					2	(SonsTemp)	
ESSEX	13	0	1	IOOF (MU)	1	(AoDruids)	15
GLOUCESTERSHIRE	14	3	2	IOOF (MU)	0		19
HAMPSHIRE	13	3	5	IOOF(MU)	0		21
HEREFORDSHIRE	3	2	1	IOOF(MU)	0		7
			1	nk			
HERTFORDSHIRE	14	1	7	IOOF(MU)	0		22
HUNTINGDONSHIRE	2	3	2	IOOF(MU)	0		7
KENT	14	26	0		1	(Gtemplars)	41
LANCASHIRE	91	1	2	ANO	1	(NatFrGdnrs)	122
			24	IOOF (MU)	1	(Gtemplars)	
			1	NATIOOF	1	(SonsTemp)	
LEICESTERSHIRE	14	0	1	Ancimp	1	(AoDruids)	22
			5	IOOF (MU)	1	(Gtemplars)	
LINCOLNSHIRE	18	12	8	IOOF (MU)	2	(AoDruids)	42
					2	(Gtemplars)	
MIDDLESEX	11	1	0		0		12
MONMOUTHSHIRE	6	1	2	IOOF (MU)	0		9
NORFOLK	14	12	3	IOOF(MU)	0		29
NORTHAMPTONSHIRE	14	7	3	IOOF (MU)	1	(NatFrGdnrs)	25
NORTHUMBERLAND	5	1	6	IOOF (MU)	2	(Gtemplars)	16
					2	(LOAS)	
NOTTINGHAMSHIRE	11	1	2	Ancimp	0		14
OXFORDSHIRE	9	4	2	IOOF (MU)	0		15
RUTLAND	1	0	0		0		1
SHROPSHIRE	11	2	2	IOOF (MU)	0		15
SOMERSET	8	2	0		0		10
STAFFORDSHIRE	11	5	5	IOOF (MU)	1	(NatFrGdnrs)	22
SUFFOLK	18	16	4	IOOF (MU)	1	(Gtemplars)	40
					1	(LOAS) (AU)	
SURREY	13	5	2	IOOF (MU)	0		20
SUSSEX	15	10	2	IOOF (MU)	1	(AoDruids)	28
WARWICKSHIRE	24	1	2	IOOF (MU)	1	(AoDruids)	28
WESTMORLAND	2	1	2	IOOF (MU)	1	(NatFrGdnrs)	6
WILTSHIRE	19	1	1	IOOF (MU)	1	(AoDruids)	23
			1	GUOOF	0		
WORCESTERSHIRE	7	1	0	1	1	(SonsTemp)	9
YORKSHIRE	93	23	5	GUOOF	4	(AoDruids)	149
			13	IOOF (MU)	5	(NatFrGdnrs)	
			1	NATIOOF	3	(LOAS)(AU)	
					1	(ROYSHEP)	
					1	(UOPD)	
TOTALS	610	216	164		53		1043

APPENDIX B
Scottish Friendly Society Records

	Local/County FS	AOF	ODDFELLOWS (type)		OTHER ORDERS		TOTAL
ABERDEENSHIRE	7	0	1	UNION	2	(Gtemplars)	10
ARGYLLSHIRE	2	0	0		0		2
AYRSHIRE	3	0	0		1	(Gtemplars)	4
BERWICKSHIRE	1	0	0		0		1
BUTESHIRE	0	0	0		0		0
CLACKMANNANSHIRE	0	0	0		1	(AfrFdrs)	2
DUNBARTONSHIRE	0	0	0		0		0
DUMFRIESSHIRE	2	0	0		0		3
EAST LOTHIAN	1	0	0		1	(AfrFdrs)	2
FIFESHIRE	0	0	0		0		0
FORFARSHIRE	0	0	0		0		0
KINCARDINESHIRE	1	0	0		0		1
KINROSSHIRE	0	0	0		0		0
KIRCUDBRIGHTSHIRE	0	0	0		0		2
LANARKSHIRE	24	0	0		1	(SonsTemp)	28
MIDLOTHIAN	12	0	1	NatIOOF	3	(AfrFdrs)	19
MORAYSHIRE	0	0	0		0		0
NAIRN	0	0	0		0		0
PEEBLESSHIRE	2	0	0		0		3
PERTHSHIRE	1	0	0		0		1
RENFREWSHIRE	7	0	0		0		9
ROXBURGHSHIRE	2	0	0		0		3
SELKIRKSHIRE	1	0	1	IOOF (MU)	0		2
STIRLINGSHIRE	4	0	1	IOOF (MU)	1	(LOAS)	6
WEST LOTHIAN	3	0	0		1	(LOAS)	5
					1	(INatFor)	
WIGTOWNSHIRE	0	0	0		0		0
TOTALS	73	0	4	0	12	0	103

APPENDIX C
Welsh Friendly Society Records

	Local/County FS	AOF	ODDFELLOWS (type)		OTHER ORDERS		TOTAL
BRECKNOCKSHIRE	0	0	0		0		0
CARDIGANSHIRE	13	1	11	IOOF (MU)	1	(OAB)	27
CARMATHENSHIRE	0	0	0		0		0
CARNAVONSHIRE	0	0	0		0		0
DENBIGHSHIRE	5	3	2	IOOF (MU)	0		11
FLINTSHIRE	8	5	2	GUOOF	1	(LOAS)	19
			1	IOOF (MU)			
GLAMORGANSHIRE	16	0	8	IOOF (MU)	1	(LOAS)	29
			2	NK	1	(AoDr)	
					1	(OAB)	
MERIONETHSHIRE	15	0	5	IOOF (MU)	2	(Gtemplars)	23
			1		1	NK	
MONTGOMERYSHIRE	7	3	1	IOOF (MU)	1	(Gtemplars)	12
PEMBROKESHIRE	3	0	0		0		3
RADNORSHIRE	0	0	0		0		0
TOTALS	67	12	33		8		124